Below: L.M.S. Class 8F 2-8-0 No 48420 waiting to leave Barnwood sidings, Gloucester while L.M.S. Class 5 4-6-0 No 44851 passes with a Christmas parcels train on December 19, 1962.

Steam in the West Midlands & Wales

B. J. Ashworth

LONDON
IAN ALLAN LTD

First published 1975

ISBN 0 7110 0653 9-108/74

Published by Ian Allan Ltd, Shepperton, Surrey, and printed in the United Kingdom by Ian Allan Printing Ltd

Introduction

Although railways have always held a fascination for me, I find it difficult to decide whether it was the locomotives of the two railway companies or the contrasting landscapes of my native county which exerted the greater pull.

West of the Severn, ancient open-cab pannier tanks threaded their way into the steep and mysterious maze of Forest railways, while on the Forest's northern edge "Bulldogs" and "Dukes" operated the rural passenger service on the line into Herefordshire, remembered for its red earth cuttings, narrow tunnels and repeated crossings of the meandering River Wye.

East of the Severn, stolid Midland 4-4-0s bowled along between the tall clusters of elms and even the smooth six-in-a-bar rhythm of the Bristol "Jubilees" barely disturbed the quiet of the Vale, although the Chalford "railcar" would sometimes try to tease them into making a race of it past Haresfield and down the straight to Tuffley. Judging from the looks I have seen on the faces of passengers travelling by the up "Devonian" a diminutive Great Western 0-4-2T propelling its single vehicle at 70mph presents quite a comic sight.

Continuing with the landscape theme, the Cotswolds provide yet another variation, particularly striking for the westbound rail traveller, who, having crossed miles of open farmland further east, is suddenly confronted with a dramatic change as the train emerges from Sapperton Tunnel and starts the long winding descent of the Golden Valley — a rather overworked title, but in this instance, it seems to me, quite apt. In particular it brings to mind frosty autumn mornings at Chalford, with perhaps the sound of a Great Western "Saint" starting its train on the 1 in 70 gradient, the echoes passing to and fro between precipitous beech woods on one side and the tiers of stone houses on the other.

With so many memories like these from the 1940s, railways and landscape were more or less inseparable in my mind, but by

1960, when I belatedly started in earnest on a photographic record, nearly all the older locomotives of character kept in service by wartime shortages had been replaced by those of more standard design. This loss was in itself an added inducement to include less of the locomotive and more of the surroundings in my railway photographs. In fact the inclusion of certain points of scenic interest became quite a challenge and produced problems, some of which proved practically insurmountable. I frequently felt the need for something like a miniature helicopter to achieve freedom of movement in the vertical and horizontal until the right viewpoint had been reached! With a top shutter speed of a 300th of a second and only one additional, rather inferior, 90mm lens, I felt better equipped for slow-moving subjects or more distant types of shot, and was usually quite happy to leave the dramatic trackside shots to photographers with more expensive equipment. Dramatic and artistic as these rail level pictures can be, some have an artificiality about them which does not appeal to me, preferring as I do the familiar, everyday view of the steam train — across fields and between trees. I usually like a high viewpoint for the way it reveals the lie of the land, the layout at a junction, or the sweep of a curve as it follows the contours; added to which it eases the task of printing, by cutting out large areas of featureless, hazy sky.

Returning again to the locomotives, there was some resurgence of interest when the diesels displaced two or three unrebuilt "Patriots" southwards to Barrow Road Depot, Bristol, to be followed by frequent appearances of "Royal Scots" on summer extras. I always think it was a pity neither of these types survived into the preservation era in their original forms. Again, during the last years of steam power a few of the bustling, small-wheeled Great Western 2-6-2Ts reappeared in the Gloucester area, after several years of absence, to work on branch line goods or the few remaining local passenger trains. On the rare occasions I was lucky enough to catch them at work they made a very welcome change from the all too numerous pannier tanks or standard Class 2 2-6-0s usually employed on branch line work.

Regarding the pictures which follow, I must say that I had misgivings when faced with the task of printing them. Spending sunny (some were, anyway!) summer days shut in a make-shift darkroom did not appeal to me, and adding yet another collection of steam engine pictures to the considerable pile of nostalgia already produced seemed superfluous. In fact it seemed to me that few lengths of track hereabouts could have escaped the cameras of the hundreds of other enthusiasts who pursued the dwindling remains of steam power in the 1960s — yet another reason for avoiding the more commonly-used viewpoints. If some stretches of line seem to have more than their fair share of pictures, it is because I feel the surroundings call for extra attention and also because my means of transport encouraged a leisurely, detailed, exploration. I nearly always cycled, then walked and scrambled to points of interest, rather than used a car, which although taking me further afield would probably have inhibited the appreciation of scenic details off the beaten track. Some urban main line scenes outside the designated area have also been included to help correct the bias towards rural branch lines.

While sorting through my negatives I was struck not only by the obvious change in locomotives and rolling stock but by the way buildings and track layout, if still existing at all are now frequently reduced or modified to such an extent that one compares the photograph and the present scene with something approaching disbelief — and all this in the space of ten years or so. Perhaps it was this speed of change which helped to make the steam engine apparently more widely popular now than when it was part of everyday life?

B. J. ASHWORTH

Churchdown,
Gloucester
January, 1975

Far left, top: L.M.S. Class 8F 2-8-0 No 48420 leaves the coaling stage at Barnwood Gloucester on December 19, 1962.

Left: L.M.S. Class 8F 2-8-0s Nos 48420, 48189 and M.R. Class 3F 0-6-0 No 43593 line up for duty at Barnwood Gloucester on December 19, 1962.

Far left, below: Barnwood shed, Gloucester on a foggy November day in 1961. From left to right: L.M.S. Class 4F 0-6-0 No 44264, M.R. Class 3F 0-6-0 No 43645, L.M.S. Class 8F 2-8-0 No 48220 and B.R. Standard Class 5 4-6-0 No 73137 with Caprotti valve gear.

Above: L.M.S. Class 4P 4-4-0 No 41123, the last of the once numerous compounds to be employed between Birmingham and Bristol, at Barnwood shed, Gloucester on May 3, 1959.

Right: G.W. 4-6-0 No 5031 *Totnes Castle* heads the southbound "Cornishman" out of Gloucester Eastgate on September 26, 1961.

BARTON STREET JUNCTION
THE CORNISHMAN
C35

Above: A B.R. standard Class 9F 2-10-0 starts away for the north from Gloucester Central on February 29, 1964.

Right: "Only a trickle after all" — G.W. 2-6-2T No 4135 at Gloucester Central on March 30, 1963.

O CROSS
MEANS
RIDGE
4135

Above: G.W. 2-6-2T No 4564 at Gloucester Central with the 10.25 a.m. to Chalford on September 14, 1964.

Right: S.&D.J.R. Class 7F 2-8-0 No 53806 skirts The Park, Gloucester, on the High Orchard Docks branch on May 12, 1961.

53806

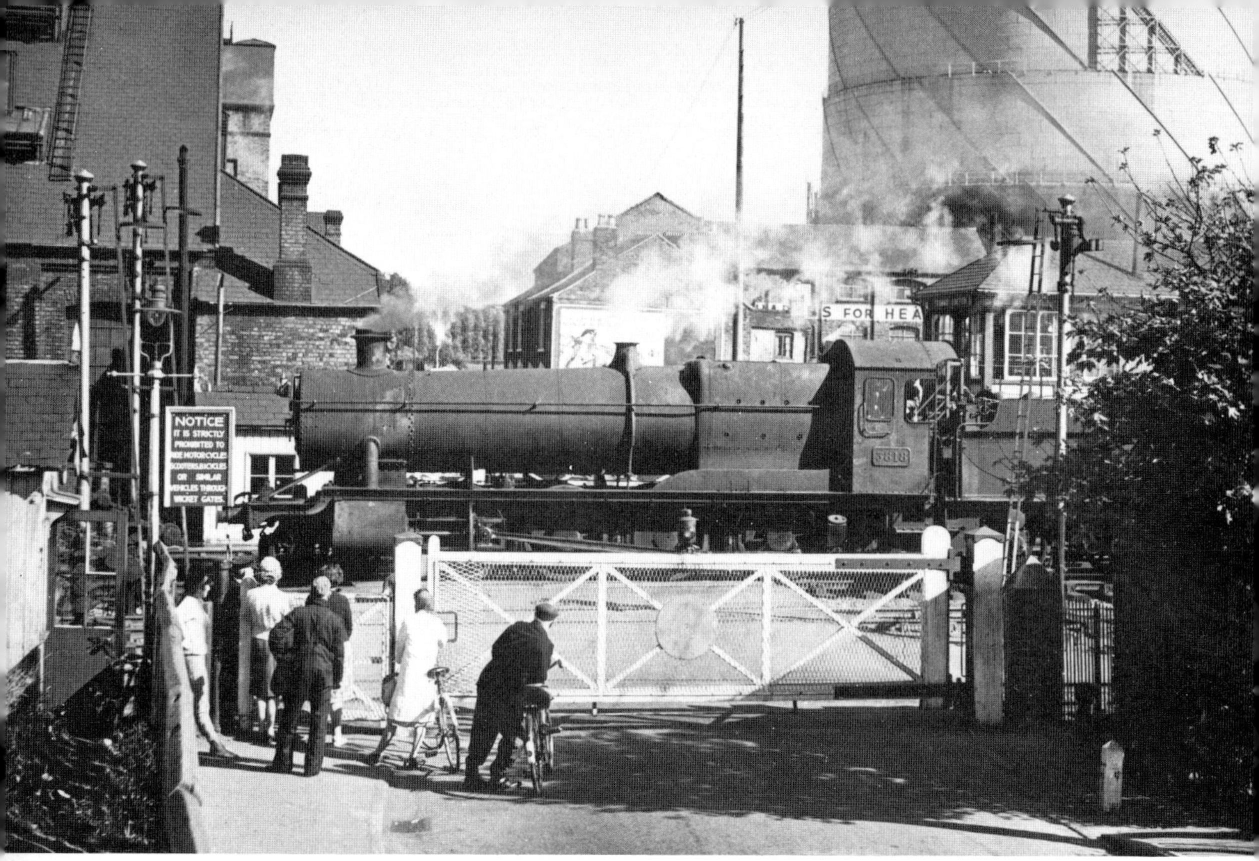
NOTICE
IT IS STRICTLY
PROHIBITED TO
RIDE MOTORCYCLES
OR SIMILAR
VEHICLES THROUGH
WICKET GATES.
S FOR HEA

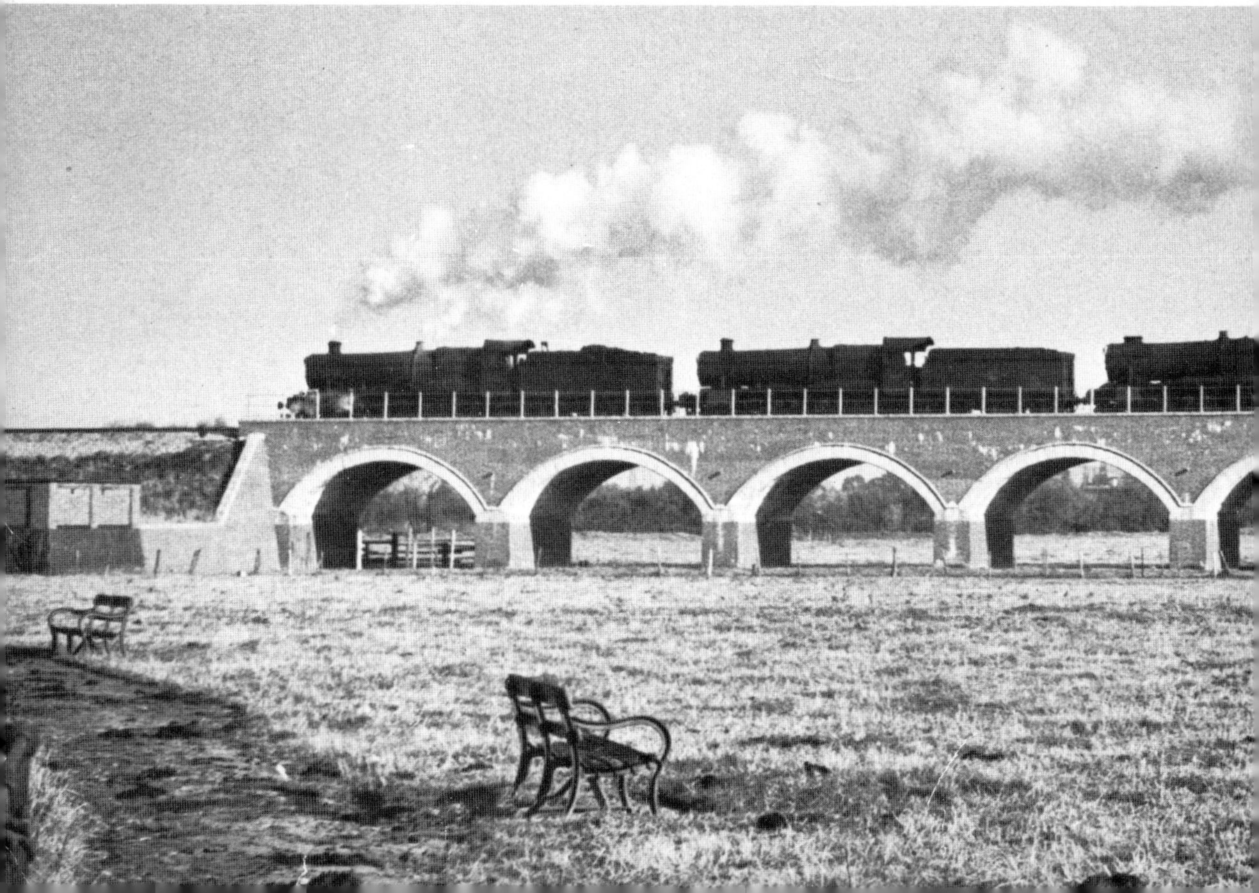

Left: G.W. 2-8-0 No 3818 at Tramway Junction, Gloucester on September 21, 1964.

Below: On October 16, 1964 two "Hall" and three "County" class G.W. 4-6-0s head west from Gloucester for the breaker's yard in South Wales.

Above: M.R. Class OF 0-4-0T No 41537 shunts at Gloucester docks on September 20, 1962.

Above left: "Austerity" 2-8-0 No 90529 crosses the River Severn at Over Junction with a freight from South Wales on November 24, 1962.

Left: On January 23, 1963, the coldest day ever recorded in the area, Class 8F 2-8-0 No 48515 approaches the frozen River Severn west of Gloucester.

Above: A G.W. 4200 Class 2-8-0T above the flood waters near Over Junction on January 25, 1962.

Right: G.W. 0-6-0PT No 8743 arriving at Docks Branch Sidings, Over, in a hail shower, with a load of Forest of Dean coal for Castle Meads power station on November 13, 1963.

Right: The centre pair of driving wheels from G.W. 4-6-0 No 5049 *Earl of Plymouth* in Barnwood shed yard, Gloucester on February 23, 1963.

Below: On New Year's Day, 1962 G.W. 4-6-0 No 6856 *Stowe Grange* passes Churchdown with the 10.15 a.m. second class-only Gloucester Eastgate-Worcester.

Above left: At sunset on May 19, 1965 a G.W. "Castle" class 4-6-0 starts from Gloucester South with a freight for Old Oak Common.

Left: G.W. 2-8-0 No 3804. November 15, 1963.

Above: New Year's Eve 1962.

Above left: Workers pause to watch a quartette of L.M.S. Class 4F 0-6-0s, Nos 43951, 44185, 44419 and 43958, at Churchdown on September 13, 1962.

Left: L.M.S. "Patriot" class 4-6-0 No 45504 *Royal Signals* heads a fitted freight for Washwood Heath past Churchdown on July 5, 1961.

Above: G.W. "Hall" class 4-6-0 No 6999, bereft of nameplate *(Capel Dewi Hall)*, passes Churchdown with the 11.22. SO Newquay-Wolverhampton Low Level on August 7, 1965.

Right: G.W. 2-6-2T No 4564 starts the 2.35 p.m. to Swindon out of Cheltenham St James on May 7, 1964.

Far left top: On the turntable at Cheltenham St James, S.R. Class U 2-6-0 No 31794 is made ready for the return working to Southampton at 1.52 p.m. on August 15, 1959.

Far left: G.W. 2-6-0 No 6365 waits at Cheltenham St James with the 3.25 p.m. to Gloucester Central on August 1, 1963.

Above: L.M.S. Class 4F 0-6-0 and Class 8F 2-8-0 return north running light past Cheltenham Lansdown Station Signal Box on April 1, 1963.

Left: Under Stanway Viaduct.

Far left: A G.W. "Hall" class 4-6-0 crosses Stanway viaduct between Winchcombe and Honeybourne with the 11.10 a.m. S.O. Ilfracombe-Wolverhampton Low Level on July 31, 1965.

Above: G.W. 4-6-0 No 6855 *Saighton Grange* at Hunting Butts Tunnel on the outskirts of Cheltenham with the 6.55 a.m. S.O. Wolverhampton Low Level-Penzance on July 31, 1965.

Left: B.R. standard Class 4 2-6-0 No 76052 arriving at Defford with a Worcester-Gloucester Eastgate stopping train on August 18, 1964.

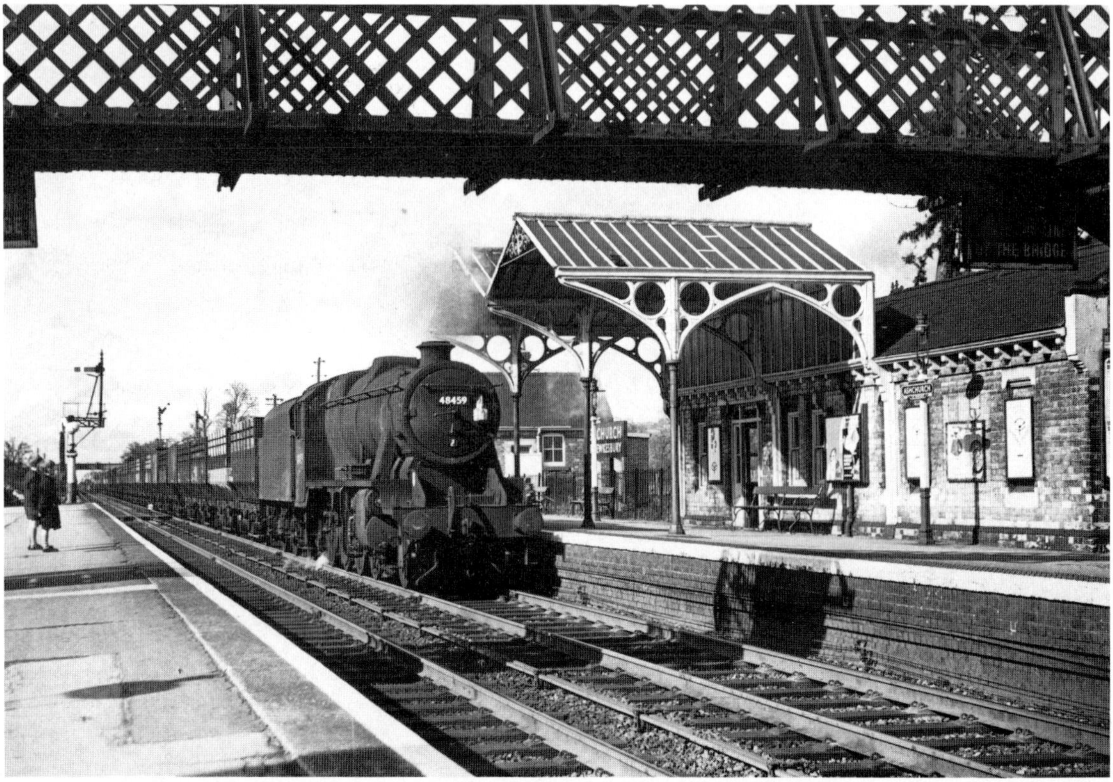
48459
CHURCH
ASHCHURCH
THE BRIDGE

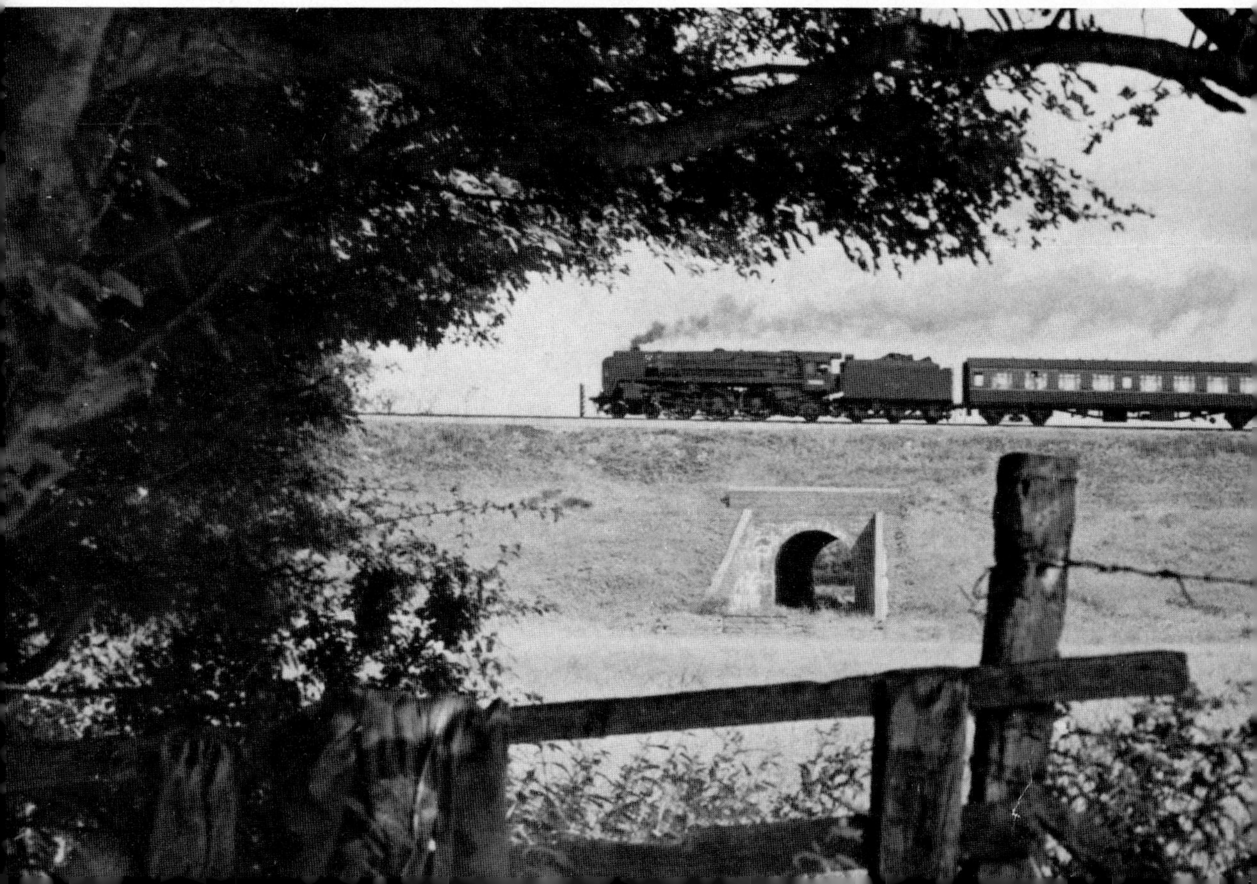

Far left: L.M.S. Class 8F 2-8-0 No 48459 heading south through Ashchurch on April 12, 1965.

Bottom: "Britannia" Pacific No 70053 near Badgeworth, south of Cheltenham, with the 8.00 a.m. SO Wolverhampton Low Level-Ilfracombe on July 24, 1965.

Left: Approaching Westerleigh West Junction on the 10.05 a.m. SO Kingswear-Wolverhampton Low Level, a G.W. "Hall" class 4-6-0 passes over the Midland line, which it is about to join at Yate South.

Below: L.M.S. Class 5 4-6-0 No 44965 approaches Haresfield with a Bristol-Gloucester stopping train on October 24, 1964.

Left: "Britannia" Pacific No 70053 crosses from 'Midland' to 'Western' lines at Standish Junction with the 11.10 a.m. SO Ilfracombe-Wolverhampton Low Level on July 17, 1965.

Below: Near Standish Junction on July 20, 1961, G.W. 4-6-0 No 7003 *Elmley Castle* on the 6.33 p.m. Cheltenham-Swindon meets G.W. 4-6-0 No 4945 *Milligan Hall* on an Acton-Margam freight.

Right: G.W. "Manor" class 4-6-0 No 7816 *Frilsham Manor* near Elm Bridge with the 5.00 p.m. Gloucester Central-Cheltenham St James on October 21, 1965.

Below right: From the goods shed at Coaley Junction, L.M.S. Class 4 2-6-0 No 43122 is seen leaving with a Bristol-Gloucester stopping train. L.M.S. Class 2 2-6-0 No 46527 waits with the Dursley branch train. The date is September 1, 1962.

Far left: B.R. standard Class 2 2-6-0 No 78004 arriving at Stroud Wallbridge on May 14, 1965. The main line station is just visible in the background.

Top: B.R. standard Class 2 2-6-0 No 78001 crosses the Thames-Severn canal at Ryeford with the branch goods for Nailsworth and Stroud Wallbridge on August 23, 1965.

Left: L.M.S. class 3F 0-6-0T No 47308 passing Woodchester on a Gloucester Railway Society Special bound for Nailsworth on July 7, 1963.

Above: B.R. standard Class 2 2-6-0 No 78004 at Woodchester on May 21, 1965.

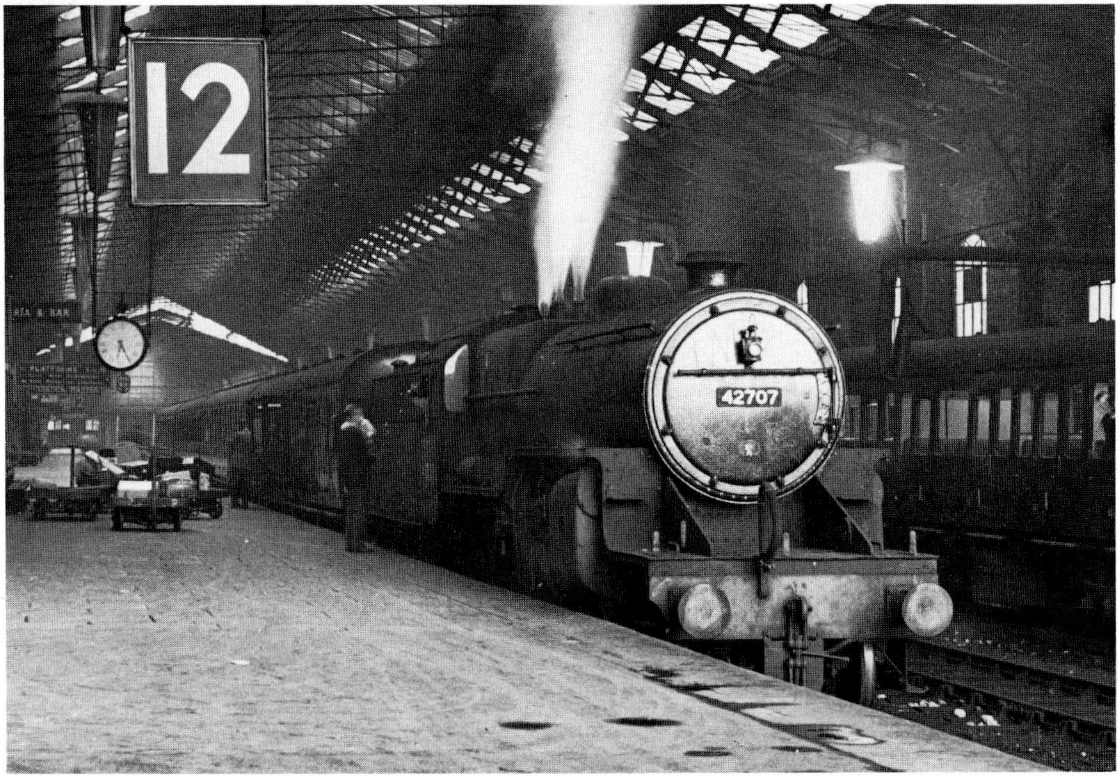

Far left, top: L.M.S. Class 4F 0-6-0 No 44045 stands in the goods yard at Nailsworth on May 7, 1962.

Far left: L.M.S. Class 6P5F 2-6-0 No 42707 at Bristol Temple Meads with the 6.30 p.m. stopping train to Birmingham on August 3, 1963.

Above: Widely differing exhaust beats echo from the surrounding trees as the down "Pines Express" nears the summit at Combe Down Tunnel, Bath on August 12, 1961. The train engine is S.R. "West Country" class Pacific No 34045 *Ottery St Mary* and the pilot, L.M.S. Class 2P 4-4-0 No 40564.

Left: L.Y.R. Class OF 0-4-0ST 51217 and S.&D.J.R. Class 7F 2-8-0 No 53810 at Barrow Road shed, Bristol on June 21, 1959.

Far left: M.R. 0-6-0 No 43754 shortly after leaving The Mythe tunnel, Tewkesbury with the Upton-on-Severn-Ashchurch branch passenger on the evening of June 19, 1961.

Below left: G.W. 4-6-0 No 7002 *Devizes Castle* stopping at Great Malvern with the up "Cathedrals Express" on May 5, 1963.

Left: G.W. 2-6-2T No 6147 runs down from the Malvern Hills towards the north end of Ledbury tunnel with a train from Worcester on June 14, 1964. A runaway line climbs the bank on the left.

Below: M.R. Class 1P 0-4-4T No 58086 at Bath Green Park on June 21, 1959.

Bottom: L.M.S. 0-6-0T No 47506 with the Ashchurch-Upton-on-Severn branch train at Ripple on July 5, 1960.

Above: G.W. 2-6-2T No 6147 leaving Ledbury with a stopping train for Worcester on June 14, 1964.

Above right: On December 21, 1963 B.R. standard Class 2 2-6-0 No 78006 takes the Dymock goods through the frost near Malswick.

Right: The Dymock branch goods near Lassington on April 11, 1962 with G.W. 0-6-0 No 2245 in charge.

Above left: M.R. 0-6-0 No 43754 crosses the River Severn at Saxon's Lode with the 5.10 p.m. from Ashchurch on June 19, 1961.

Left: G.W. 2-6-2T No 6155 produces a smoke ring at Tunnel Junction, Worcester. B.R. standard Class 4 4-6-0 No 75005 is arriving from Hereford. The date is May 9, 1963.

Above: G.W. 0-6-0PT No 1661 with spark arrester chimney shunts between the locomotive sheds at Worcester on May 9, 1963.

Above: Worcester shed yard on May 9, 1963.

Right: G.W. 4-6-0 No 7005 *Sir Edward Elgar* heads eastwards from Evesham under the Ashchurch-Redditch line on May 9, 1963.

Far right: G.W. 4-6-0 No 7002 *Devizes Castle* about to leave Worcester with a Hereford-Paddington train on March 15, 1963.

DEVIZES CASTLE

Right: A Paddington-bound train headed by G.W. 4-6-0 No 7011 *Banbury Castle* about to enter the Cotswold edge at Campden Tunnel on July 2, 1962.

Below: G.W. 4-6-0 No 7007 *Great Western* makes a brief stop at Kingham with a Paddington-Hereford train on July 2, 1962. G.W. 2-6-2T No 4101 has just returned from Chipping Norton and will continue on to Cheltenham.

Far right: G.W. 2-6-2T No 4101 crosses the main line at Kingham as it arrives from Cheltenham on July 2, 1962. B.R. standard Class 2 2-6-0 No 78001, with fire recently dropped, stands outside the shed. The Chipping Norton branch curves away to the right.

Far right, bottom: On a stormy day in February 1962 a brief flash of sunlight crosses the Cotswold top at Notgrove station. G.W. 2-6-2T No 5182 is about to start its train downhill to Bourton-on-the-Water.

Above: Andoversford Junction on September 29, 1962 with G.W. 2-6-2T No 5184 pulling away from the station on a train for Kingham. The M.&S.W.J. line diverges to the right.

Left: Cheltenham (Leckhampton) on September 27, 1962 with G W. 2-6-2T No 4142 on an afternoon train for Kingham.

Above right: G.W. 2-8-0 No 2872 at Withington, Glos, during recovery of track from the M.&S.W.J. line on August 19, 1963.

Right: The same locomotive as seen from the derelict signal box.

Far left: S.R. Class U 2-6-0 No 31626 runs down into the Colne valley near Withington with a Southampton-Cheltenham train on June 28, 1961.

Above: In the Cotswolds near Cassey Compton, a Stephenson Locomotive Society Special hauled by G.W. 4-6-0 No 7808 *Cookham Manor* marks the end of the passenger service between Cheltenham and Southampton on September 10, 1961.

Left: G.W. 0-6-0PT No 1664 with its Tetbury branch brake-van rests in a sunny spot at Cirencester Town station, on April 24, 1964.

92204

Left: *King George V* in Swindon shed on October 21, 1962.

Below, far left: The chimney from *County of Chester* in Swindon Works on October 21, 1962.

Below left: A B.R. standard 9F 2-10-0 in Swindon Works on October 21, 1962.

Right: Near Frampton Mansell on February 14, 1962, G.W. 2-6-0 No 5380 has stopped to pin down brakes on a westbound freight. G.W. 2-8-0 No 2886 rounds the corner on an up freight, with steam from the banking engine rising over an intervening ridge.

Below: On January 22, 1963 G.W. 4-6-0 No 4980 *Wrottesley Hall* passes Frampton Mansell with G.W. 2-6-2T No 5184 at the rear.

Above: G.W. 4-6-0 No 7021 *Haverfordwest Castle* passing Frampton Mansell with the 9.05 a.m. Paddington-Cheltenham on December 12, 1961.

Right: G.W. 4-6-0 No 7034 *Ince Castle* heads the "Cheltenham Spa Express" up Sapperton bank on June 5, 1962.

Far right: B.R. standard Class 4 4-6-0 and G.W. 2-6-2T No 5182 climb through sunshine and shower at Chalford on July 15, 1961.

Far left: A G.W. "Castle" class 4-6-0 climbs past Chalford on August 3, 1961.

Above: G.W. 2-8-2T No 7203 and 2-6-2T No 5173 start away from Brimscombe on March 18, 1961.

Left: At Brimscombe on August 2, 1962 G.W. 2-8-2T No 7228 heads west alongside the Thames-Severn canal.

Above: G.W. 0-4-2T No 1420 returning to Leominster from Kington past Bullocks Mill crossing on August 20, 1964.

Top right: The last westbound 'Cornishman' leaves Cheltenham Malvern Road on September 7, 1962 behind 'Castle' Class 4-6-0 No 7001 *Sir James Milne*.

Right: Class A4 No 4498 *Sir Nigel Gresley* heads south from Dinmore Tunnel on the Shrewsbury-Newport secton of an A4 Locomotive Society tour on October 19, 1974.

Above: G.W. 0-4-2T No 1426 on the Gloucester-Chalford auto-train pulls out of Brimscombe past banking engines Nois 4101 and 4116 on February 14, 1962.

Left: G.W. 0-6-0PT No 8471 near Ham Mill Halt with an evening Gloucester-Chalford train on September 15, 1964.

Below: G.W. 0-4-2T No 1453 approaching Stonehouse with the Chalford auto-train on October 24, 1964.

Above: The evening Bromyard-Worcester branch passenger train leaving Knightwick behind G.W. 0-6-0PT No 8793 on July 28 1964.

Left: Scene of dereliction at Titley Junction in September 1964.

4573

Left: WR 2-6-2T No 4573 on a Ledbury branch train in Lassington Wood on June 20, 1959.

Right: At Abergavenny on September 5, 1963 G.W. 2-8-2T No 7206 waits to assist a "Western" class diesel towards Llanvihangel with the 11·00am Plymouth-Manchester.

Below: SR Class U 2-6-0 No 31795 of Eastleigh shed at Chedworth on a through working to Cheltenham over the former MSWJ line from Southampton on March 22, 1960.

Above: B.R. standard Class 4 2-6-0 No 43106 of the Severn Valley Railway crossing the River Severn north of Bewdley on May 30, 1974.

Left: Unloading the goods from Worcester at Bromyard on June 24, 1964.

Right: G.W. 0-6-0 No 2242 at Eardisley on August 19, 1964. Disappearing into grass in the distance is the section formerly continuing to Hay and Three Cocks Junction.

WR 'Castle' Class 4-6-0 No 5017 *The Gloucestershire Regiment* heads up the Golden Valley near Frampton Mansell with a morning express from Cheltenham to Paddington on October 3, 1959.

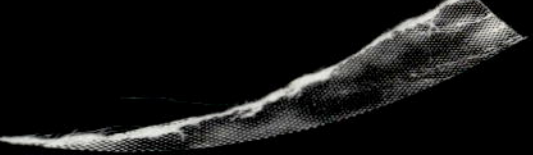

Far left: 1420 at Presteigne on August 13, 1964.

Far left, below: *King George V* approaching the split level tunnels at Dinmore on the Hereford-Shrewsbury section of a Wirral Railway Circle tour on October 5, 1974.

Left: Preserved "Jubilee" 4-6-0 NO 5596 *Bahamas* takes over from *King George V* at Hereford with an L.C.G.B. special on October 14, 1972.

Bottom: G.W. "Castle" class 4-6-0 No 5061 *Earl of Birkenhead* pounds past Llanvihangel with a Manchester train on October 28, 1961.

Facing page top: LM Caprotti Class 5 4-6-0 No 44753 pilots 'Jubilee' Class 4-6-0 No 45664 *Nelson* through Churchdown on a Cardiff-Newcastle express on July 22, 1961.

Far left: Near Pontardulais on August 17, 1970 an NCB 0-6-0ST heads up the valley towards Craig Merthyr Colliery.

Above: Class 3F 0-6-0T No 47308 after arrival at Nailsworth, on the branch from Stonehouse, with a railway enthusiasts' excursion on July 7, 1963.

Left: At Upper Soudley in the Forest of Dean on October 12, 1960 — WR 0-6-0PT No 8701 hard at work.

Above: G.W. 0-6-2T No 5691 approaching Abercynon with a train for the Merthyr line on September 23, 1964.

Above right: At Ffaldcaiach on August 26, 1964 G.W. 0-6-2T No 5621 waits to assist a freight arriving from Ystrad Mynach.

Right: N.C.B. 0-6-0ST *Sir Gomer* shunts his shedmates around the shed yard at Mountain Ash on May 28, 1974.

ALL DOWN
STOP DEAD
9K05

Above: Another view in the Golden Valley, on the climb from Stroud into the Cotswolds: WR 2-6-2T No 4101 assists 4-6-0 No 5951 *Clyfe Hall* up the bank near Frampton Mansell on August 17, 1959.

Above right: W.R. 0-6-0PT No 4671 climbs past Netherhope Halt on March 11, 1965 with empty hoppers for Tintern quarry on the Wye Valley line.

Right: B.R. standard 9F 2-10-0 No 92122 pulls out on to the main line at Bullo Pill Box, south of Newnham, on September 24, 1965. In the foreground is the sand drag at the foot of the Cinderford branch incline.

15

Above: Dereliction at Maerdy in July 1972.

Above right: A gap in the N.C.B. fence at Maesteg in July 1974.

Right: N.C.B. 0-4-0ST *Clydach* shunts the exchange sidings at Pontardulais on August 21 1970.

Far right: The N.C.B. shed at Maesteg in July 1974.

9642

Above: G.W. 0-6-0PT No 6437 at Sharpness on May 17, 1963.

Above right: A northbound freight headed by G.W. 4-6-0 No 6995 *Benthall Hall* crossing the River Wye at Chepstow on March 11, 1965.

Right: A westbound freight headed by G.W. 4-6-0 No 6948 *Holbrooke Hall* skirts the River Severn at Purton on April 18, 1964.

Right: On April 18, 1964 G.W. 4-6-0 No 5971 *Merevale Hall* heads a freight from South Wales past the Severn railway bridge.

Below: G.W. 2-6-2T No 5518 makes a rapid getaway from Sharpness South Signal Box on December 13, 1963.

Bottom: A Stephenson Locomotive Society special with G.W. 0-6-0PTs Nos 6437 and 8701 in charge, negotiates the sharply curving 1 in 30 past Point Quarry on the Coleford Branch on May 13, 1961. The former tramroad route passes under the line on the extreme right of the picture.

Top: Push-and-pull-fitted G.W. 0-6-0PT No 5420 in the repair shop at Lydney on June 23, 1962.

Above: Coleford Junction on July 2, 1964 and G.W. 0-6-0PT No 3728 arriving from Lydney with empty hopper wagons bound for Whitecliff Quarry.

Right: With driving wheels spinning, G.W. 0-4-2T No 1445 makes an unsuccessful attempt to draw its load of scrap metal forward on to the main line and across to the Severn & Wye branch at Berkeley Road on July 20, 1964. G.W. 2-8-0s Nos 4701, 2852 and 2842 are bound for the docks at Sharpness.

BERKELEY

Far left, above: On May 25, 1965 S.&D.J.R. Class 4F 0-6-0 No 44560 passes Berkeley Loop Junction Signal Box with a Sharpness-Gloucester goods containing an atomic flask.

Far left, below: G.W. 0-4-2T No 1445 arriving at Berkeley from Sharpness on April 16, 1964.

Above: With wagon brakes pinned down, G.W. 0-6-0PT No 8701 eases its load round the reverse curves at Darkhill on the Coleford branch on April 13, 1962.

Left: G.W. 0-6-0PT No 8745 between Bilson Junction and Cinderford Station on March 29, 1965, with the Whimsey and Churchway branches visible behind. The embankment between is the site of the former Severn & Wye branch to Cinderford.

Above: On January 14, 1965, G.W. 0-6-0PTs Nos 8745 and 9711 stand outside the tunnel approaching Whitecliff Quarry on the former Monmouth & Coleford Railway.

Right: G.W. 0-6-0PT No 8749 leaves Bradley Hill Tunnel at Upper Soudley on August 28, 1964.

BERRY
BERRY
FETTER LANE

Left: G.W. 0-6-0PT No 3775 on the Whimsey branch near Cinderford on July 22, 1965.

Above: Teatime at Longhope in November 1963.

Below: G.W. 0-6-0PT No 3775 takes water at Bilson Junction before propelling empties to Northern United Colliery on July 22, 1965.

Left: The 10.25 a.m. Hereford-Gloucester about to enter Lea Line Tunnel headed by G.W. 2-6-0 No 7318 on September 22, 1964.

Top: A Gloucestershire Railway Society Special between the tunnels at Lower Soudley on June 23, 1962, headed by G.W. 0-6-0PT No 6424.

Above: G.W. 0-6-0PT No 9676 passes Pentir Rhiw on the long climb to Torpantau on September 4, 1963.

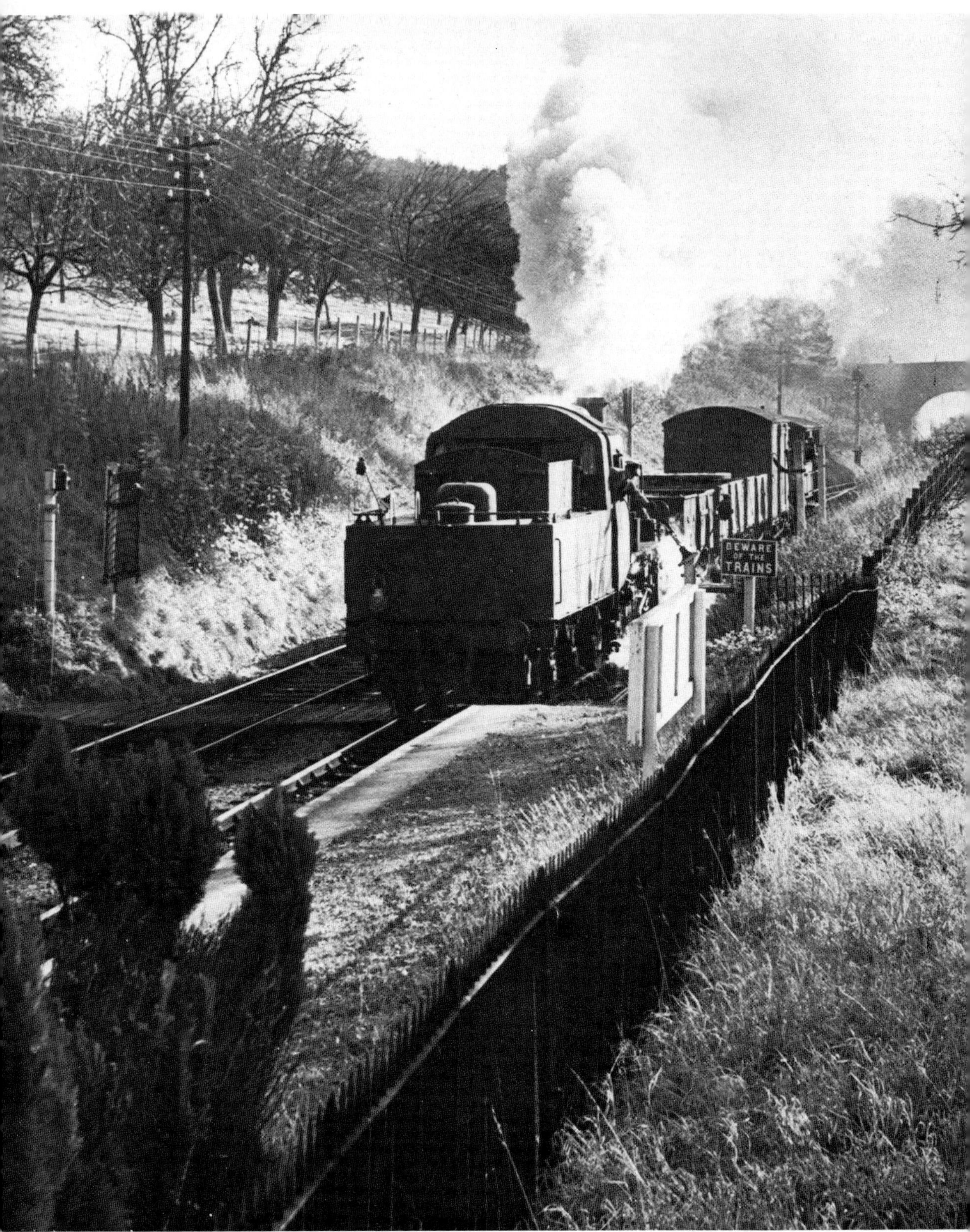
BEWARE
OF THE
TRAINS

Left: B.R. standard Class 2 2-6-0 No 78004 passing Longhope with the Gloucester-Hereford goods on November 26, 1963.

Above: The Grange Court Junction signalman takes the single line token as a Hereford-Gloucester train joins the main line on April 24, 1964.

Above left: On October 17, 1964 the 12.10 p.m. Gloucester-Hereford climbs away from Longhope.

Far left: G.W. 2-6-0 No 7319 approaching Mitcheldean Road with a Hereford-Gloucester train on August 7, 1964.

Left: Shortly after leaving Ballingham the 1.25 p.m. SO Hereford-Gloucester crosses the River Wye on July 4, 1964.

Above: At Lydbrook Junction on April 14, 1964 G.W. 0-6-0PT No 3728 shunts the former Severn & Wye branch.

Right: G.W. 2-6-0 No 7319 approaching Backney Halt, west of Ross-on-Wye, with a train for Hereford on June 22, 1964.

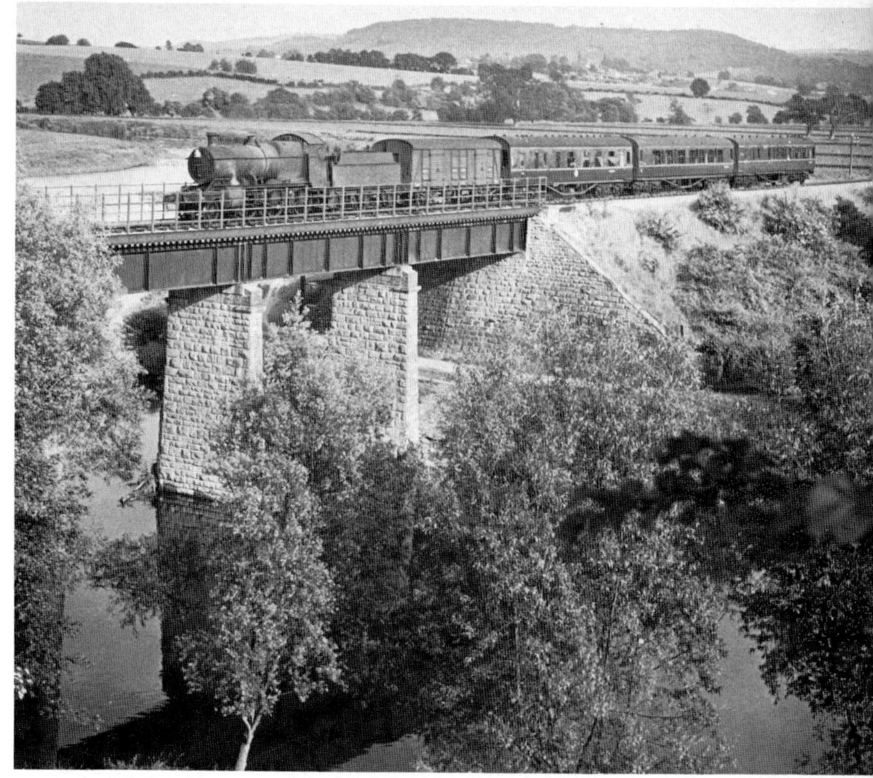

Above: Llandrindod Wells on June 5, 1964 with L.M.S. "Jubilee" class 4-6-0 No 45577 *Bengal* arriving on a Shrewsbury train.

Right: Early morning at Ross-on-Wye on September 24, 1964.

Far right, above: L.M.S. Class 5 4-6-0 No 45406 crossing Knucklas Viaduct on May 16, 1964 with the 11.45 a.m. Shrewsbury-Swansea Victoria.

Far right: Within sight of Offa's Dyke, the 9.45 a.m. Swansea Victoria-Shrewsbury, hauled by L.M.S. Class 5 4-6-0 No 45154, crosses Knucklas Viaduct on May 16, 1964.

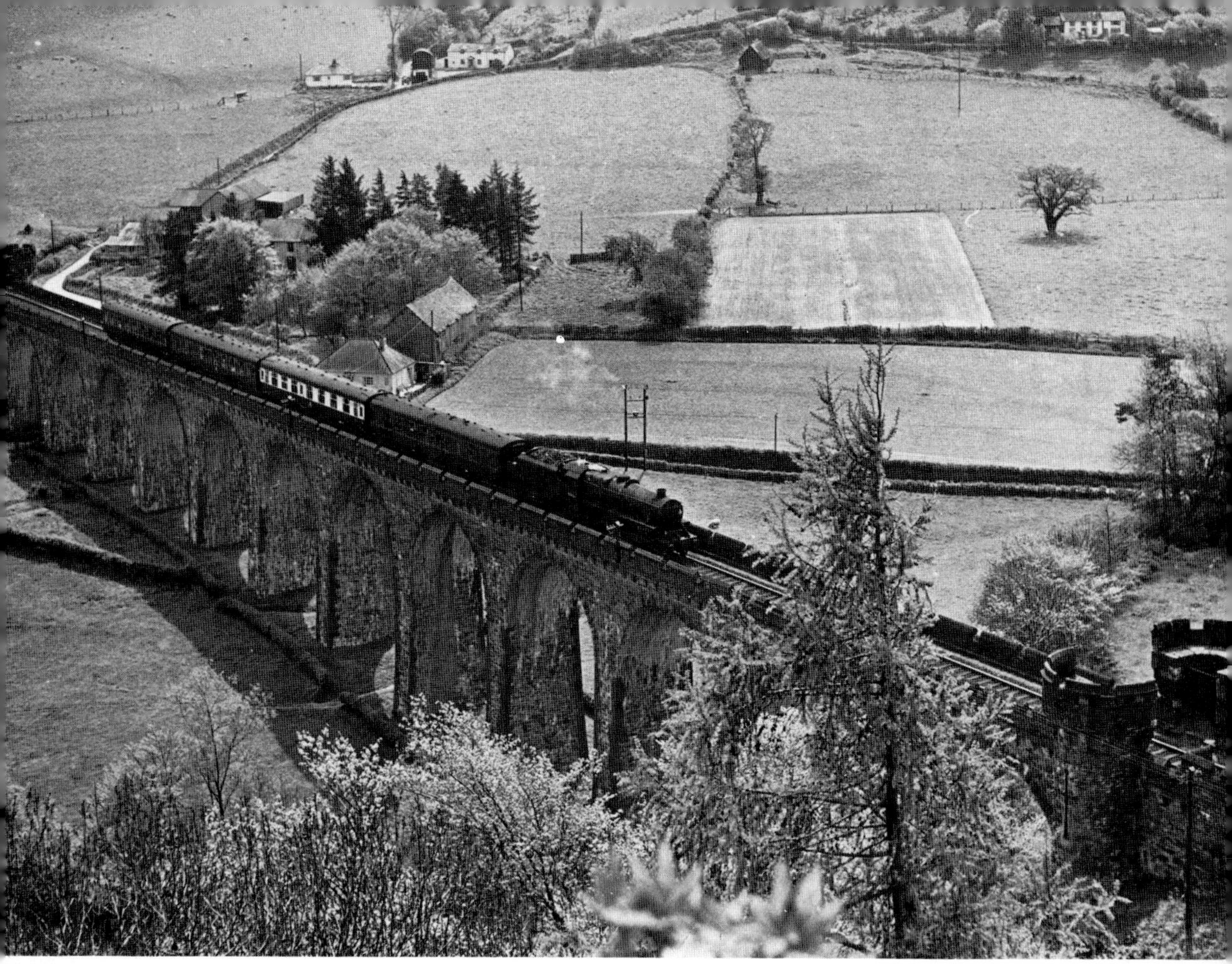

Below: Early morning on the Sugar Loaf and an L.M.S. Class 8F 2-8-0 climbs out of the frosted lowlands with the Llandovery-Craven Arms pick-up on October 30, 1961.

Right: B.R. standard Class 4 2-6-4T No 80069 takes water at Knighton with the 2·40 p.m. Shrewsbury-Swansea Victoria on June 2, 1964.

Far left: At close on 1000ft above sea level in the Radnorshire hills L.M.S. Class 8F 2-8-0 No 48369 heads south from the summit tunnel near Llangunllo on May 16, 1964.

Above: Two L.M.S. Class 8F 2-8-0s, Nos 48409 and 48524, head south over the River Wye near Builth on August 29, 1962.

Left: At Builth Road High Level station on June 4, 1964 L.M.S. Class 8F 2-8-0 No 48328 and crew rest for a while. Approaching from the south is Class 5 4-6-0 No 45145 with a Shrewsbury train.

Right: L.M.S. Class 2 2-6-0 No 46520 on the 12.30 p.m. Builth Road-Brecon, following the River Wye between Aberedw and Llanfaredd on August 25, 1962.

Below: At Builth Road on August 29, 1962. L.M.S. Class 8F 2-8-0 No 48354 arrives with a Shrewsbury train while L.M.S. Class 2 2-6-0 No 46516 waits in the Low Level station with the connecting 1.20 p.m. Brecon-Moat Lane.

Far right: On October 30, 1961 two L.M.S. Class 8F 2-8-0s climb towards Sugar Loaf tunnel on the Carmarthen-Brecon county boundary.

Below right: Three Cocks Junction on August 23, 1962. From left to right the 1.20 p.m. Brecon-Moat Lane, 12.30 p.m. Builth Road-Brecon and 12.42 Hereford-Three Cocks.

Far right, below: Talyllyn Junction station in September 1963.

Above: Talyllyn Junction station in September 1963.

Top: Under the easternmost peak of the Brecon Beacons the 11.15 a.m. Newport-Brecon descends the 1 in 38 from Torpantau with G.W. 0-6-0PT No 3706 in charge, on November 11, 1962.

Right: G.W. 0-6-0PT No 9618 crosses the Brecon and Newport canal at Talybont-on-Usk with an engineers train after dismantling of signalling equipment at Talyllyn Junction on September 1, 1963.

Above: View from the 11.15 a.m. Newport-Brecon, arriving at Talyllyn Junction on August 23, 1962. L.M.S. Class 2 2-6-0 No 46516 is waiting with the 1.20 p.m. Brecon-Moat Lane.

Left: G.W. 0-6-0PTs Nos 9676 and 4690 stop in the drizzle at Talybont-on-Usk with the last regularly double-headed Brecon-Merthyr goods on August 30, 1963.

46170

Left: At Torpantau on August 30,1962, G.W. 0-6-0PTs Nos 3747 and 4611 meet on the 11.15 a.m. Newport and 12.10 p.m. Brecon.

Below: The rebuilt L.M.S. experimental high pressure 4-6-0 *Fury,* No 46170 *British Legion,* starting from Birmingham New Street for Euston on August 18, 1962.

Right: L.M.S. "Jubilee" class 4-6-0 No 45670 *Howard of Effingham* running into Birmingham New Street on August 18, 1962.

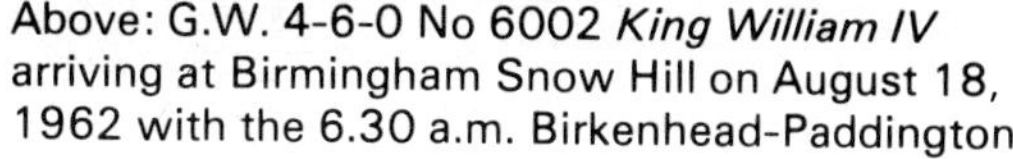
Above: G.W. 4-6-0 No 6002 *King William IV* arriving at Birmingham Snow Hill on August 18, 1962 with the 6.30 a.m. Birkenhead-Paddington.

Above: LMS "Jubilee" class 4-6-0 No 45579 *Punjab* starts a Pembroke Dock-Derby train from Birmingham New Street on August 10, 1963.

Right: Birmingham Snow Hill: "King" waiting.

Far right: Birmingham Snow Hill: "King" leaving.

V02

Above: B.R. standard Class 4 2-6-4T No 80101 and G.W. 4-6-0 No 7821 *Ditcheat Manor* after arrival at Dovey Junction from Pwllheli and Aberystwyth with sections of the "Cambrian Coast Express" on June 11, 1963.

Right: L.M.S. Class 5 4-6-0 No 45272 heads north from Birmingham New Street on August 10, 1963.

Far right, above: The Aberystwyth section of the "Cambrian Coast Express" headed by G.W. 4-6-0 No 7821 *Ditcheat Manor,* as seen from the Pwllheli section, approaching Dovey Junction on June 11, 1963.

Far right: B.R. standard Class 4 4-6-0 No 75002 swings around the continuously curving stretch of line following the Dovey estuary between Penhelig and Gogarth Halts on June 15, 1965.

Above left: Over the top at Talerddig, G.W. 4-6-0 No 7812 *Erlestoke Manor* starts the long run down to Cemmes Road on June 3, 1965.

Left: A pair of 2-6-2Ts at Towyn Wharf on June 8, 1963: Welsh Highland Railway *Russell* and B.R. standard Class 3 No 82032.

Above: Between the tunnels at Penhelig Halt, B.R. standard Class 3 2-6-2T No 82033 pulls away with the 3.45 p.m. Machynlleth-Pwllheli on June 19, 1962.

Top: An evening train from Machynlleth runs down to the dunes near Aberdovey station behind B.R. standard Class 3 2-6-2T No 2000 on June 19, 1962.

Above: At Morfa Mawddach on June 7, 1963 B.R. standard Class 4 4-6-0 No 75006 is about to take the Ruabon line with the 10.20 a.m. Barmouth-Birkenhead.

Right: The Pwllheli section of the up "Cambrian Coast Express", headed by B.R. standard Class 4 4-6-0 No 75002, follows the steep coastline between Llangelynin and Tonfanau on June 14, 1965.

9

Left: Vale of Rheidol Railway 2-6-2T No 9 *Prince of Wales* is prepared for work outside the former standard gauge shed at Aberyswyth on August 7, 1969.

Below: Talyllyn Railway No 6 *Douglas* in the wall-papered shed extension at Pendre on August 6, 1968.

Top: A Rheidol Valley train climbs towards Devils Bridge on August 6, 1969.

Above: Aberystwyth shed on June 9, 1964. B.R. standard Class 4 2-6-4T No 80136, Class 3 2-6-2T No 82009 and G.W. 4-6-0 No 7828 *Odney Manor.*

Right: Vale of Rheidol 2-6-2T No 7 *Owain Glyndŵr* heads up-river towards Capel Bangor on August 8, 1969.

Right: Talyllyn Railway No 2 *Dolgoch* returns to Pendre shed after providing banking assistance up to Cynfal on June 6, 1965.

Below: Talyllyn Railway No 2 *Dolgoch* crosses Dolgoch viaduct with a down train on August 6, 1968.

Far right: On the Talyllyn Railway at Bryn Glas on August 8, 1968 No 1 *Talyllyn* waits for No 6 *Douglas* to pass with a down train.

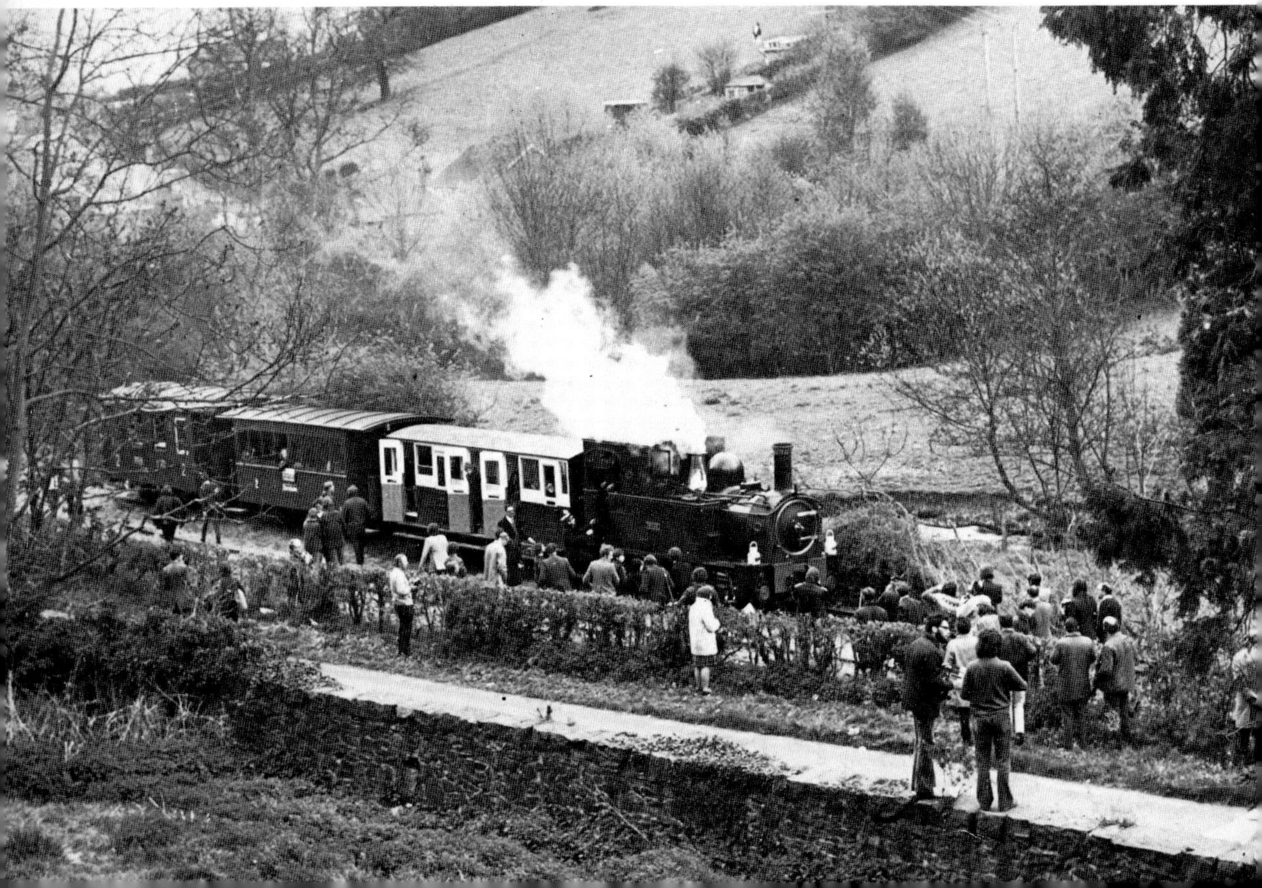

Above left: *Linda* runs downhill towards Penrhyndeudraeth with a Festiniog Railway train on August 27, 1974.

Far left: *The Earl* at the Welshpool terminus on May 12, 1973, with a members-only special to commemorate the 70th anniversary of the opening of the Welshpool and Llanfair Railway.

Above: Welshpool and Llanfair 0-6-0T *The Earl* crosses the River Banwy on August 2, 1968.

Left: Austrian 0-8-0T *Sir Drefaldwyn* approaching Heniarth Halt on the Welshpool and Llanfair Light Railway on August 21, 1974.

Above: A Festiniog Railway double Fairlie passing Boston Lodge on June 11, 1965.